Polymer C

The Ultimate Beginners Guide to Creating Animals in 30 Minutes or Less!

Table of Contents

Introduction

First and foremost I want to thank you for downloading the book, *"Polymer Clay: The Ultimate Beginners Guide to Creating Animals in 30 Minutes or Less!"*

In this book you will learn how to create your own polymer clay animals. You are going to learn everything you need to know before you ever begin working with polymer clay, including what you need to know in order to choose the correct clay for you. You will learn what tools you will, need and then you will learn how to create cute polymer clay animals.

You will be taught step- by- step how to create each animal, and at the end of the book you will be given tips to help you work with polymer clay. When you have finished with this book you are going to be able to create your own projects and make all different types of polymer clay creations.

Thanks again for downloading this book, I hope you enjoy it!

Chapter 1

Getting Started With Polymer Clay

You have probably seen some amazing creations from polymer clay, and now you're excited to get started making your own creations. The first thing you should know is that you do not need to run off to the craft store and pick up a ton of supplies, which is good news. There are a ton of little supplies you can purchase and most of them cost very little, but if you go out and purchase a bunch of things you will not need, the cost will add up quickly.

In this chapter we are going to go over what you will need, starting with how you will choose your polymer clay. Many different things need to be considered when you are choosing which brand of polymer clay to purchase. One is what the clay contains. Some clay may contain ingredients that you are allergic to, and that is something you need to check before you purchase any clay.

Next you will need to consider color. Color differs with each brand. When you first start out using polymer clay you may work with a few different brands. It is best if you make a small color chip out of each color you purchase, and label the color chip before you cure it. Meaning you will put the brand of the clay on the chip and the color or number of the color for future reference.

By doing this you will be able to learn which colors change on you after they have been cured. For example, some reds may become almost black once they have been cured. If you use this color on a project that you want a bright red on you will be disappointed, but by using color chips you will know exactly what the results will be each time.

Make sure you make your chips the same size and thickness. Consistency does matter when it comes to how your clay will turn out. It is not reliable to use one chip that is 1mm thick and compare it to how a chip that is a .5 inch ball. These are not comparable.

The next thing you need to consider is the structure of your clay. Some brands are going to be much softer than others which mean it is very easy to work with, but since clay gets softer in the oven before it hardens you will need to prop up any parts of your animal that may bend or fall over; such as a horn or leg.

Other clays are harder to work with but hold up well in the oven so you have to decide what your preference is. And there are also clays that are so soft you have to let them sit out in the air for a little while so they become a little harder before using them. This will allow your clay to become the right consistency to work with.

You also want to consider if you are going to be building a base with the clay and covering it with different clay. For most of the projects I do that are larger, I use aluminum foil to create a base and cover it with clay. Some people like to create a base with one type clay and cover it with another. If you are going to create your base with clay you will want to purchase something cheap, like a kid's polymer clay and cover it with a more expensive one.

With all of this information how are you supposed to choose which polymer clay is right for you? The best advice I can give you is to go out and purchase a few different brands and play with them a little bit, then choose which one you like working with the best. If you have hand problems you will probably want to go for softer clay, but if you prefer harder clay you will know which brand to purchase.

The next thing you will need is a working surface. You cannot just use your kitchen table for this. There are two reasons, one: polymer clay is known to stain any porous surface and should not be used in areas where you prepare food. Second: polymer clay will pick up even the tiniest crumb or hair you miss when cleaning, and it will ruin your project.

Instead you should go purchase a simple white ceramic tile. This can be purchased for about 50 cents, and you can create your project and bake it on the tile.

You will need some acrylic paint, roller, paint brushes, toothpicks, glue, spoons and knives. If you need other items for specific projects you can pick them up along the way. Make sure if you use anything out of your kitchen you keep it separate and don't use it for food preparation later.

A few other items you will need is: razor blades, not the kind you shave with but the actual blade inside the razor, an x-acto knife, as well as something to smooth your clay with. You need something more than your finger because this leaves finger prints. A small spoon will do when you are just starting out though.

You can make a ton of different projects out of polymer clay but for the remainder of this book we are going to focus completely on how to make different animals. Some of these will be life-like, and some will be creative, but all of the colors are simply a suggestion. You can use whatever colors you prefer.

Chapter 2

Polymer Cat

The first thing we are going to learn is how to sculpt a simple polymer cat. This cat will be about the size of a quarter when we are finished. Of course if you want to make your cat bigger just start off with a larger ball of clay, but most of the polymer clay projects will remain small like this one.

Start off with a ball of black clay. Using your hands shape the ball into the body. It is best if you can look at a picture of the animal while you are shaping the body out of the clay if you really want to make it look realistic.

Once you have the body shaped, you will want to take four small balls of clay and roll them out to legs. Attach the legs to the body and smooth out the joints. If you want to make your cat sitting down simply make paws for the back legs and for the front, bend the legs in any shape you want.

After you have the legs smoothly attached to the body, you are going to bend a small portion at the bottom to create the paws. You can use your toothpick to make the details in the paws.

While you are working on your cat, you really want to focus on building up the muscles if you are trying to make the cat look real. On the other hand, if you just want a cute little cartoon inspired cat you don't have to worry about the muscle structure as much.

After you have your legs and paws created exactly how you want them you will roll out a small ball and create the tail. Makes sure you smooth out the seam where the tail connects to the cat's body and bend the tail to your liking.

Roll out another ball to create the cats face, and attach another smaller ball where the nose should be. You will smooth this ball until you get the correct shape for the cat's nose. Using the tip of a glue bottle you can create the indents for the cat's eyes. Of course you can use any tool you want for this.

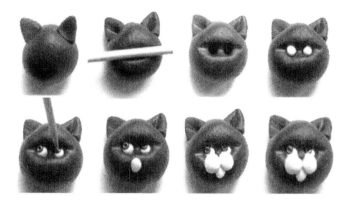

There are tools that are made for using with polymer clay that have a ball on the end, some of them are larger than others but the smaller ones are great for creating indentions for eyes and the larger ones are great for smoothing out clay and creating muscle tone. Now grab your toothpick once again and create the nose holes for the cat as well as the cat's mouth. If you want to add some thin black wire for whiskers you can use your tooth pick to create very small, thin holes or you can use the wire. Do not add the wire now just create the holes. After the cat is baked you will put a bit of glue on the end of the wire and place it in the hole.

Next you will need to cut out two triangles for the ears. Attach these to the cat's head and smooth out the seams. Take two small balls of white clay and create the eyes with a bit of green and black clay as well. You can place these in the eye sockets now, but I find that they usually fall out when baking, instead place them on your tile and let them bake separately using glue to add them to the cat's face later.

Now your cat is ready to bake. Another way of creating a cat and making easier to pose is to create a structure for the cat out of wire.

You will create a loop where the head will be, and create a structure for the cat's body, tail and legs. If you want to use less clay you can build onto this structure with aluminum foil and then place small pieces of clay on top of the foil. Smooth it out as you go, but make sure the structure is in the position you want your cat to be in before you cover it with foil.

If you want to add fur to your polymer clay cat after it has baked you will purchase a bit of mole fur or faux fur. Using a paint brush you will add a little bit of glue to each area of the cat gluing the ends of the fur to the cat. This takes a little bit of time since you can only do small areas at a time, and you have to make sure that the ends of the fur attach to the cat.

Once you have covered the entire cat with fur or the areas you want you will need to give you your cat a haircut trimming the fur back to a length that looks natural for the cat.

Watch This Cool Video on Making A Halloween Polymer Clay Cat!

Chapter 3

Polymer Clay Koi Fish

Koi fish are so cute, and they are so much fun to make out of polymer clay. One great thing about this project is that you can simply stick an eye pin through the fish before you bake it and create cute charms or necklaces.

You will need white polymer clay, translucent polymer clay, black polymer clay, red polymer clay and orange polymer clay. Or whatever colors you want your fish to be. You will also need some type of rolling pen; if you do not have a rolling pen made for using with polymer clay a simple marker will do the job.

If you want to make it a charm you will need eye pens, and if you want to glaze the fish you will need some glaze for polymer clay.

The first step in making this polymer clay koi fish is to create the body of the fish. All you need to do is take your white polymer clay or whatever color polymer clay you want your fish to be and create a tear drop shape out of it.

Once you have the tear drop shape you will want to take the smallest part of the tear drop and slightly curve it. Of course this is optional, but it gives the illusion of the fish swimming in the water.

The second step is to create patterns on your koi fish. You will want to set the body of your koi fish to the side, take your rolling pin and roll out the first color of clay you want to add to your koi fish, this could be the red, orange or black (or the color you have chosen).

You are going to roll this out very thin. It will end up being about as thin as tracing paper when you are done with it.

If you have ever seen a koi fish, you will notice that the patterns are not shaped in any specific way. In order to get this effect you are going to tear the polymer clay instead of cutting patterns out. You want to make sure it has a bit of a jagged, uncut looking edge.

Just tear off small pieces of the polymer clay and place it on your fish wherever you want it. You will repeat this with all of the colors that you want your koi fish to have on it. You will want to make sure that you do not cover the entire fish but leave some space in the front where the face will be.

The next step is creating the fins and the tail. In order to create the tail, you want to roll out your translucent polymer clay to the thickness you would like, place your fish on the clay and mark the width of the back of the fish on the translucent polymer clay with a toothpick. This will simply give you a starting point for your tail. After you do this, you need to take your knife and cut out the shape of the tail you want.

Some people prefer their koi to have long flowing tails, while others simply cut out a small cute tail. Connect the tail to the body smoothing out any seams and add any details you would like. You may also like to add a few different colors to the tail like you did to the fish's body. It is completely up to you. Bend the tail in the shape that you want it, and it is time to cut out the fins.

You will once again roll out your translucent polymer clay, and cut small triangle fins out. Then place them to the side of the fish.

Another way to do this is to use tiny balls of polymer clay, flatten them out and use one half of the circle for each fin.

Using your knife, you will add the lines on the fins just like you did on the tail. Now you can add the final fin, the Dorset fin on top. Simply roll out your clay, and cut your clay out to the shape you want. You will want to add any lines to this fin before you attach it. After you have added the lines, simply attach it to the top of the fish.

You can also use glue to attach these, but I have found that it is unnecessary and actually makes things harder. You want to make sure the top fin curves with the shape of the fish.

Next you want to take two tiny balls of black clay and create the eyes. Simply flatten these onto the face of the fish. If you want to create a charm, now is the time to add a pin. Bake the fish according to the directions on the pack of your polymer clay.

Once the fish has finished baking you will add your glaze if you choose to do so. Let the glaze dry, and your fish is complete. You can also create mini koi fish ponds out of these fish to sit up in your house. Add them to necklaces, bracelets and earrings to create cute jewelry.

Click Here to Watch This Tutorial on Making a Clay Koi Fish

Chapter 4

Polymer Clay Sheep

In this chapter we are going to learn how to create a simple polymer clay sheep. All you are going to need is white polymer clay and black polymer clay.

First roll out a thin line of white polymer clay and cut it the width of two fingers. You will want to create a lot of these small strips and twist them up into curls for your sheep. Do this by simply taking one end of the strip and curling the rest of the strip around it.

Now you will create an oval shaped body for the sheep out of white polymer clay and attach these curls to the body creating its wool. If you want to save your polymer clay, you can use some foil to create the base for the body and cover the foil with clay. You will find that by doing this you are using less than half of the clay you would have, had you created the entire body out of it.

While you are adding the curls over the body you want to leave one end not covered so that you can add the sheep's head. Don't worry about leaving an area that is too large, you can always add more curls later.

If you want to create a short haired sheep, you need to roll out some white clay into a long thin line like you did for the last sheep. Instead of cutting it in sections of two finger widths, you will want to cut small pellets out of it. Eventually you will end up with a pile of these small pellets.

Take the body of the sheep, whether created entirely out of polymer clay or out of foil covered in clay, and roll it around on the pellets. As they attach, simply flatten them out a little bit attaching them better to the body. Once the body is covered you are ready to move on to the next step with both sheep.

Now you will need to make some flat oval eyes out of white polymer clay. Flatten them after you have made the ovals.

Grab your black polymer clay and roll out a snake. You will cut four hooves from this so it needs to be a bit thicker than what you made the wool out of. Roll out a tail, and create the ears for the sheep.

You will also use the black clay to shape the head of the sheep. You will want to create oval shapes that are proportional to the rest of the body. On one end of the oval you will place the ears, and then add the white ovals for the eyes.

Make one hole on each side of the nose of the sheep and use your X-acto knife to create a mouth. Use two tiny circles of black polymer clay and create the pupils for the eyes. Place the head on the body. If you need to add more wool or short hair now is the time that you should do so.

Place the tail on the back of the sheep and the hooves on as well. You can add detail to the hooves, and you will do the exact same thing to both of the sheep.

After you have created both of your sheep you need to bake them according to the directions on the back of your polymer clay. Once they are baked you can add glaze to them or keep them as they are. These are not meant to look like real sheep. They are cute sheep that are more cartoonish than they are real, but they are very cute and a lot of fun to create.

I hope that you have been able to create the projects we have worked on this far. Most of these have been very simple, but the more you work with polymer clay, the easier it will become for you to add more and more details. There will come a time when you won't even need help creating projects.

One of the best tips I can give you: If you want to create realistic looking animals get a picture of the animal to look at while you create it. Using pictures as a reference is a great way to learn.

You will actually want to get several pictures because you will need one from many different angles. You also want to make sure that you get pictures of the same breed of animals. For example if you want to create a beagle, a picture of a poodle is not going to help you create the shape of a beagle. The same goes for different breeds of horses.

One last thing about these sheep, when you are adding the black pieces as the head, tail or hooves, you may find that you are getting black smudges on the white wool, this can be very annoying, but it is very easy to deal with.

One way you can deal with any smudging of colors is by using a polymer clay cleaning technique. You don't have to purchase anything for this. Just get a small cup of water and some q-tips.

Dip the q-tip in the water and rub it on the smudged area. This will remove the smudge. Only use one q-tip per area, and make sure you do not use too much water. Too much water can ruin your entire project. So if the water is dripping off of the q-tip remember it will drip all over your project as well.

This is something that took me a long time to learn and has been a life saver of many of my projects. I will share more tips like this in the final chapter of this book, but for now let's move on to our next project.

Watch This YouTube Tutorial on Creating a Clay Sheep

Chapter 5

Polymer Pig and Turtle

The last two projects we are going to learn are: How to create a cute polymer clay pig and a turtle. For the pig, you will need which ever color of pink clay you want to make your pig.

To begin you will need to roll out a circle of clay for the body, of course you can use foil for this and just use clay to cover the foil if you wish. You will need one circle of clay for the head, two small black circles for the eyes, a small circle of clay for the nose, a small snake of clay for the tail, two small circles of clay for the ears and four small circles of clay for the feet.

You will want to take the piece of clay you have for the body and start to form it into a tear drop shape. Make sure the head is a circle and attach it to the smallest end of the tear drop shape. Take your piece of clay you have for your nose, roll it into a ball and flatten it into an oval shape.

Place this on the pig's face. Next is the ears, you want to roll the clay for the ears into a ball and flatten it into a triangular shape. You want both of the ears to look very similar so you may want to make both before attaching them.

You will not be blending the seams of this pig. You are not working with a lot of detail at this point so you can leave the seams as they are.

Attach the ears to the pig and bend the clay creating the ear shape that you want. You can fold it slightly forward to create an ear flap if you want.

Next you will want to put the eyes on, so take your two black balls of clay and place them on the face of the pig just above the nose. Take your tool and make two small holes in the nose of the pig finishing up the detail on the nose.

Roll out your tail to the thickness you want it and curl the tail. Remember that pigs do not have long tails so one and a half small curls is usually enough. Attach this to the back of your pig.

Make each of your balls of clay for the feet into a small tear drop shape attaching the smallest part of the tear drop to the pig's body. You can use black to do this if you wish since pigs do have hooves, or you can use pink. Again, it is completely up to you. Now your pig is done. If you want to add an eye pin to create a charm you will do it at this point. One thing I like to do is get creative with my pigs is add a splash of mud to them.

Remember when we were adding color to our koi fish? You can add a bit of mud to your pig using the same process. Simply roll out your brown clay until it is about the thickness of tracing paper. Tear off sections creating a jagged edge and lay it on your pig creating slashes of mud.

You can also use black to add patterns to your pigs because if you have ever seen a pig you know that many of them have black patches on their skin. It all depends on how realistic you want your pig to look and how much time you are willing to put into your pigs.

You can create a bunch of them to sit up or add them to jewelry. No matter what you do these are very cute as well as fun and easy to create.

Now let's finish up by creating a polymer turtle. I am going to give you the basic steps to create your turtle. Then you can make your turtle on your own by adding the details that you want to it.

For any turtle, no matter what size you choose to make it, you will need a piece of brown clay for the shell or whatever color you choose, one piece of green clay for the head, four pieces of green clay of equal size for the feet, a small piece of green clay for the tail and two tiny pieces of black clay for the eyes.

Of course these colors are just suggestions, and you should use whatever colors you like the most. You can also use very small pieces of white clay to add a bit of detail to the eyes.

First you will want to shape your shell. You will want the top of the shell to be shaped like a mound and the bottom to be flat. You can add a rim around the shell if you would like, or just leave it as a mound.

Next you will take the piece of clay you have for the head of the turtle and shape it however you would like. You can make it a thin oval or a fatter circle depending on how you want your turtle to look.

Attach this to the shell of the turtle. Take the tail of the turtle and shape it into a tiny candy kiss shape or little tear drop and attach it to the back of the shell. Roll the clay for the legs in between your fingers and flatten both of the ends. Attach this to your turtle.

Now you can add any detail to your turtle's shell that you would like and to any other part of the turtle, for example: His feet. Once you have done this, you will attach the eyes of the turtle. Grab a tooth pick and make two small holes for his nose, and you are ready to bake.

Chapter 6

Tips You Need To Know When Working with Polymer Clay

I want to finish off this book by sharing with you a few tips that you should know when you are working with polymer clay.

1. Hand sanitizer will remove any residue left on your hands from working with polymer clay. You should use this whenever you change the color of clay you are working with so that you are not leaving one color residue on another color and ruining your projects.

2. Never use nail polish when painting polymer clay. It will dissolve you clay. Many people do not know this, and they will try to use clear nail polish as a glaze on their projects only to find out later they have completely ruined their work.

3. You can make soft clay harder by placing it between two sheets of paper and placing a book on top. The paper will draw out the moisture from the clay, but you want to make sure you don't leave it for too long or your clay will crumble.

4. You can soften up hard clay too! Simply add a bit of baby oil to your polymer clay and work it in well to make your hardened clay softer.

5. Many people will tell you that you can decorate your creations with sharpie markers; you can draw on the eyes or add whatever you want after the project has baked, but sharpie

marker will just fade when you use it on polymer clay. Over time your creation will no longer have any eyes or features if you use sharpie marker.

6. If you want to keep your polymer clay in the best condition store it in a simple zip lock bag. These will keep the air from your clay, and the plastic in the bags does not react with the clay causing it to ruin unlike some bags.

7. Don't invest a ton of money when you are first starting out. You may find that you do not really enjoy working with polymer clay, and you don't want to waste money on purchasing items you will never use. Instead purchase a few items, try to make a few creations like the ones you learned in this book and decide if working with polymer clay is right for you.

Creating animals out of polymer clay can be a lot of fun, and it can also become frustrating, which is why I did not focus too much on creating life like animals in this book. When you first start out you want to make creations that are fun for you but cute as well. You don't want to take on a huge project such as a large horse, work hard and end up giving up in the end because you didn't take the time to learn how to make simple projects.

Learn simple projects first and then move on to harder projects with more detail, but make sure that no matter what you are doing, you are having fun while you create your projects.

[Check Out The Awesome Video on YouTube That Helped Me Out A Ton When I First Got Started Working With Polymer Clay!](#)

Conclusion

Thank you again for downloading this book!

I hope this book was able to help you to learn how you can start creating polymer clay animals on your own.

The next step upon successful completion of this book is to take on some harder projects or create some of your own. Use your imagination and see what you can create.

Finally, if you enjoyed this book, please take the time to share your thoughts and post a review on Amazon. It'd be greatly appreciated!

Thank you and good luck!

Bonus Chapter: Get Started With Paper Mache

Chapter 1: The Tools of the Trade: Everything you need to know in order to get started.

Before we get into paper mache, it would properly be a good idea to actually know what paper mache actually is about. The word paper mache roughly means chewed paper in French. This is fitting as the substances you work with do occasionally resemble mashed up paper. Paper mache can be summarized as the act of combining paper and paste or flour and using these two basic substances to create unique and cool looking figurines. This type of craft has quite a long history, with its basic mechanisms being used in hundreds of years ago in China in the formation of helmets and with the process eventually spreading to Europe where it was practiced in France and England in the 17-19th centuries in the making of wares. You too can celebrate this historic craft by making your own paper mache figures and products. In the first chapter, we will kick things off by gifting you with the tools of the trade. We will list the necessary equipment that every good paper mache novice should be familiar with and also the two chief methods used during a typical paper mache session.

Paper mache is an inexpensive and simple activity, so you will not have a lengthy list of items you will need to purchase or a whole host of jargon and complicated instructions that you will need to memorize. There are only a few items needed and a couple of pieces of valuable information to be aware of before setting out on your paper mache adventure.

This is the great thing about this type of craft; you don't have to have immense art skill or be a Picasso facsimile or have a whole array of expensive art equipment. You just need a pair of hands, a rich imagination and a few inexpensive and easily obtainable items.

Equipment

This is a list of the equipment you will need in order to paper mache.

- **Paper:** This is usually in the form of newspaper, but you could also use magazine paper, tissue paper or just plain white computer paper. It is basically up to you and your particular preferences. But just be aware that some paper will be hardier than others, for example, tissue paper will be quite hard to use and properly will not form a stable foundation. The paper that you decide upon will need to be ripped up into long strips. This is what you will use to create your paper mache masterpiece.

- **A bowl:** This is what you will use to mix your paste or flour mixture.

- **Glue or flour mixture:** Similar to the paper, what you decide to use as your adhesive substance depends upon you. For the glue mixture, you will need to mix a portion of 2/3 white glue with 1/3 cold water in a clean bowl. This mixture will need to be stirred thoroughly until the consistency is to your preferences. However, it should not be too thick. Others prefer to use the flour method.The flour concoction can be made by placing a cup of flour in a clean bowl. Into this flour, cold water should be carefully and slowly poured until it has reached a consistency that is preferable. If it is too thick add more water and if it is too runny add a few more teaspoons of flour. There should be no lumps in your flour mixture, so make sure to stir quite vigorously. Both of these adhesive methods work well and again it is up to personal preference.

- **Paint and a paintbrush**: Paint will be needed when it is time to decorate your paper mache creation. You don't want a newspaper themed dog or pig, rather you want an eye-catching and captivating pink pig or spotty dog. Paint makes your creation just a little bit more special.

- **An extra paintbrush:** This extra paintbrush will be needed in order to mix the glue or flour mix.

- **A balloon:** An inflated balloon is often used for the foundation—what the paper is glued upon to create the paper mache figure. Once the structure has been made, the balloon is simply popped. Other foundation items can also be used, such as a specific cardboard shape.

- **Your creativity:** This is properly the most vital piece of equipment needed for this project and thankfully you don't have to go too far to find it----you already have it lying in wait internally. The process of creating a paper mache sculpture is not supposed to be a chore nor a mechanical process where you methodically put pieces of paper onto the surface of a balloon with a somber expression on your face. This is supposed to be enjoyable. So remember to have fun while doing this and use your imagination when creating your pieces.

The methods

There are two chief methods that can be used when paper mache, firstly the paper/glue method and secondary, the pulp method.

Paper/glue: The paper and glue method is what is traditionally used for the bulk of the paper mache process. This is what creates the broad foundations of your creations using glue and strips of newspaper which are stuck on a balloon or other base item.

Paper mâché is quite an easy activity to carry out. Detailed below is the complete paper mâché process, from start to finish. This will hopefully make the whole process easier.

1. Make your glue or flour paste. Set this aside for the moment.

2. Next, tear up newspaper into long strips. There should be a decent amount of newspaper used as you will properly require a bit.

3. When you have your two main components sorted out, the paste and the newspaper, you can begin to paper mâché.

4. Dip a strip of newspaper into the paste and stick in onto your foundation. Complete the process until every bit of the surface is covered. You should aim to do several layers of paper mâché so that it is stable and not flimsy. After each layer, allow time for it to dry. If

you wish for a blank and clear surface to paint over, you should make the final layer with white computer paper.

Pulp Method: The pulp method is used for the more delicate and intricate aspects of your sculpture. So when you have a section that needs a gentler touch, the pulp method would properly be favored over the glue/paper technique. This method involves making a pulp that is then spread over the paper mache form. Below we have listed a series of instructions on how to make this pulp:

Tear newspaper up into small pieces. These pieces shouldn't be too large or minuscule in size. They should be around 2-3 cm in length and width.

1. Place these pieces of newspaper into a bowl and pour hot water over them. All the newspaper should be covered with water. Leave to soak for a couple of hours or overnight if possible.

2. Once it has finished soaking, get your fingers into this mixture. Play around with it---squeezing, stirring and mushing it until it resembles a soggy mush of paper. There should be no lumps. If there is add more water to the mix and stir until it is lump free.

3. Add a pinch of salt. This is to make sure that it does not glob together. And then mix once more.

4. Next grab handfuls of this squashy mix and squeeze out any excess water over the sink. Return the drier pulp back to the bowl.

5.Lastly, add a few tablespoons of white glue to this mix and stir. A pulp has now been created which you can use while you paper mache. This mix can be stored for a few days in the fridge in an airtight container.

For both of these methods, it is important that you lay newspaper out on your working surface. You should also wear old clothes that you don't mind getting messy because paper mache is a messy business

Printed in Great Britain
by Amazon

14965919R00031